# THE AGE BEGINS

*Oneal Walters*

THE AGE BEGINS by Oneal Walters

Copyright © 2005 The Age Begins Books

Publisher's Cataloging-in-Publication Data
Oneal Walters
THE AGE BEGINS by Oneal Walters

ISBN: 0-9738573-0-7

1. Love 2. Poetry 3. Young Adults 4. Nonfiction


Published by: The Age Begins Books
www.theagebegins.com

Printing: Instant Publisher

Cover Art: Christina Wald

Printed and bound in Canada

# Table of Contents

# THE AGE BEGINS

# Love

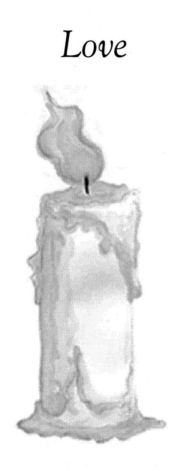

# Long Anticipation Needs Attention

I *watch her*
*Her lips, she's kiss-able,*
*I listen to her*
*Her ideas, she's adaptable.*

*I pull her to the corner.*
*My hands roll up her shirt,*
*I lift her breast out of her bra*
*Massage her caramel.*
*I touch it with two fingers*
*Light, small circles around it.*
*Her nipple swells.*
*I slowly rub it.*
*She steps away.*

*She makes a fist*
*And rubs her chest*
*Tightly over her heart,*
*"My heart is pounding pounding*
*This is too much for me." She says.*

# Born Again

"I'm behind you
Whatever you need
I'll support you.
But nothing from my pocket
Will be used to promote your book."

He accepts my ideas and creations
But won't advise me or promote it.
He expands my avenues as a poet
But does nothing for a young writer.
Word of mouth sells books,
Sign copies and gets interviews.
He sits and watches.

Different publishers reject my mail
Passing on what's ambitious.
They publish cold poems
Prefer bronze poets.

T.A.B accepts me.
A dreamer turns poet
Becomes their first writer.
I hold each poem together
And force a friction out of non-fiction.

## Passionate

He's mistaken.
Spirit to spirit connection
Through words on pages,
I highlight and fold pages
Revisiting ideas, settings
And characters months later.
I demand the best flavour.
I'm aroused by interactions.
Accept or dislike characters,
Aware of their moods.
Books are the medium,
Spirits gather to these pages.
Perhaps this is what you call 'talking,'
Perhaps when unseeing writers write
Books become loveless.
The best avenue for reviving
Breathless books is to
Breathe in the outward
Cries of people.

# Finding Pleasure

Poetry journals,
Magazines
I read them both.
I search for words
Through themes
And enter scenes
With interacting characters,
They struggle in their world.
It's like watching a movie
Seeing the performance
Feeling the emotion.
But it's not adulterated
By sub-characters.
Each person contributes,
It's a creative union.
This works perfectly
When poems like labels
Stick to spirit on contact.
It's not easy to find this.

# Same Way

*I had a fascination with libraries*
*Reading poetry journals.*
*Now I subscribe to issues*
*Reading and circling page numbers.*

*I had to admire Layton,*
*His writings lure my spirit.*
*Now I have two of his books*
*Rereading them often.*

*I had to love Ms. Angelou*
*She's honest, brave*
*And very strong.*
*Her writings are historical.*
*Now I have her poetry book,*
*I feel her words within me.*

## Really Close,
## So Far

I'm not calling her cell,
Not adding another message.
She's outside of Canada, on a trip.
It's been three weeks
Without hearing her voice.
I sit by the phone,
No ring, no answer.
The lights are off.

---

I remember her face.
Her head tilting upwards
Her long black hair
Her blinking right eye.
A tight white and pink shirt,
She's sitting on a wooden desk
She rubs her chest,
She can't breathe.

---

I look at the phone
Pick up the receiver
Hear the dial tone,
Hang up.

# A Special Proceeding

*This proceeding*
*Is not by the Publisher*
*Or the Publishing Company (T.A.B)*
*This is the express view of the writer:*

*Attention, attention*
*Thank you all for reading,*
*This is a special moment for us.*
*I have an envelope from Oneal.*
*(He opens the envelope*
*Pulls out the letter)*
*It reads:*
*"The title of my next poem*
*A Seeing Generation."*

17

# A Seeing Generation

W. H. Auden wouldn't understand my generation,
These poems give strength to the ambitious
Many accept these words and push 9 to 5 second.
A few did escape broken families healing their sight.
The middle class makes everything happen.
Auden just wouldn't understand.

W. H. Auden wouldn't understand my generation,
These poems give warmth to females
Who were 'Unloved Cargo'
And now find love.
These females must be complete
To attract and keep another's love.
Auden just wouldn't understand.

# Flourish Please

Sexuality equals popularity
avoid this, a disrespectful plot,
it loots and spoils our females.

She thinks:
uninterested American society.
I must be sold like clothing
its talent versus beauty.
Isn't this always the solution,
the reason you adore me?

Will you answer me?

He thinks:
it's truly not me versus you
not male versus females,
not watchers versus objects,
it's objects magnifying ideas,
she's attractive only by shape.
It's understanding and seeing
a healthier depiction,
this will flourish much more.

## Industry Predator

You prey in our markets
Have us pay from our pockets.
Anthologies, more anthologies.
"Show off your talent to your friends."
Our words precise, a pianist keys
We share our music globally.
We always for hire but you spoil it.
I'll flush your magazine in the toilet
Or ask a flourishing female to burn it.
I'll remove no more from my wallet.

# Wonder Now

The people don't receive your poems
And your age isn't the problem
    The reality of being older
Doesn't decrease your art,
Your reality is of questions
Your world has no answers.
I see through your images
    And you depict fear.

The people don't receive your poems.
Sympathy can't replace quality
    Tears can't sell your books.
Money, we won't earn it to lose it.
That book, only you will read it.

The people don't receive your poems.
A writer's role can't be to blind
And since you have no answers,
    You are my new question.
Spin in a circle if you like
    Fade into a failing role
It's time to go.  Wonder now.

# A Strong Female

*I'm on that bus*
*Emotions jumping*
*Over weaker emotions,*
*Their legs built to leap*
*Like grasshoppers' legs.*
*I'm near the last stop.*

*She's a pond of intelligence,*
*My mind scoops like a bucket*
*Her depth of understanding.*
*She reads novels*
*And lives in Aurora.*
*After classes we meet.*
*She tells her friend to wait*
*And spends time with me.*
*We head to the stairs.*
*As we kiss and rub each other,*
*We listen to hear if anyone*
*Comes from above or below.*

*This is not marriage,*
*It's the stop before that,*
*It's appreciation and respect.*
*This is not passion,*
*She likes her steady job*
*Prefers to follow orders*
*Wants a normal life.*
*I ring the bell.*

*This is not a single smile,*
*Not a single kiss on her lips.*
*She's a female who meets me,*
*Mentally gives and has no dreams.*

*I'm on that bus*
*Emotions jumping*
*Over weaker emotions,*
*Their legs built to leap*
*Like grasshoppers' legs.*
*I walk through a crowd*
*I exit before that stop.*

# Never, Never More

*I find myself quite weary*
*I speak aloud to myself,*
*"Never, never more."*

*Poems about 'peddled shores'*
*People in faceless conversations.*
*No identity within their characters*
*No urgency in reading more.*
*I'm spitting on their landscapes.*
*Green descriptions in poetry,*
*Forget it.*
*I push through another week*
*CV2 is coming in the mail soon.*

# Continue

Someone whispers to me,
"I'll tell you
If you don't know."
He never comes to help
And doesn't offer it again.
So I get the information.

Someone asks to participate.
He receives a small duty,
Quickly answering,
"I'll do it in two weeks,
I have too many things to do."
So I do it in an hour.

I'm not a burden to flesh.
My concerns expose answers
And I confront personal trials.
I see assistance as a gift.
But I'm not helpless.

# Separate Ways

She sits on the bench
I sit beside her
She moves to a second bench.

She looks at me,
I look at the street.
I see a couple laughing,
Sharing intimate looks.

I sit on the second bench
A lot of space is between us.
We sit in a park under a tree
Flies swarm my face.
I swat at a group.

She says, "You're wrong.
Girls and guys can be friends
Without sexual motives."
I disagree, "Females are not
My friends, well except one
But that's something else."

*She looks away,*
*I look at my watch.*
*First time meeting her,*
*Why did she come? To talk?*
*Talk on the phone at home.*
*"I have to go." I say.*
*"You just got here." She says*
*"I have things to do." I say.*
*We hug then I leave*
*"Bye."*

## Explain Love

To explain love
I would have to explain life,
Life is to be in constant giving
To strive to lift up another.
To welcome another's success
But not allow it to threaten
Your own success.
Love must be seen, felt
Not constantly told
Though much is given
When one is clearly told.
To love is not to be broke
Or be a slave to another,
To love is to inspire, heal
And to embrace
The innermost parts
Of the spirit one wants to please.
To love is to share
To bear one's spirit
And as naked, expect
To be clothed by another.

# Giving and Receiving

I like us together
Disagreements a few
No fighting
Money always shared
Giving without counting.
A lot of jokes,
A lot of personal jokes.
Problems we absorb,
My pain is yours
Your pain is mine.

I'll see you tomorrow,
We'll talk for a while
And in a private place,
I'll give you warmth.

# Trustworthy

Now the book sales
Sway my way,
Overcome with T.A.B,
I will today.

Overcome he did yesterday.
Layton his intense intimacy
His female characters
I admire his poetry.

## Lonely Spirits

*Soft sweet gentle girl*
*Slowly holding kissing*
*Each, in darkness, other*
*Hotel window blinds closed*
*Night falling on us*

*Worries, separate story*
*Upset mother angry*
*Strange boy alone, danger*
*Daughter, maybe holding kissing*
*Boyfriend? Alone room, possibly*

# Love or Weakness?

*I open your mind*
*Exposing you to my world.*
*Now suddenly naked.*
*I want to scream out,*
*I shared ¾ of my secrets!*

# Explain Touch

To share is to anticipate hurt,
To watch another not receive
What you offer to them freely.
To touch is to take without concern,
To know exactly what you need
Without questioning another's view.

I touch her smoothness
And excite her with my fingers.
We stand in a doorway in a shadow
My back is towards the university hallway,
My words seduce her and we kiss.

To not share is to accept defeat,
To lose a battle that gives growth.
To not touch is to abandon experience,
To know exactly what you need
But never willing to take to succeed.

# Oneness

She has his chain on
As if that makes them married.
They have oneness and openness,
She observes his strengths and weaknesses
From a height of safety.
He debates his reality,
What he is chosen to be
Versus who is he is currently.
She bends and watches him
As he finally decides.
She listens to his dreams and efforts,
She listens to his clues that includes her
Into his future efforts and she smiles.
She relies on their conversations
And depends on his ideas.

## What I Love

Stay with me
Sit
Listen to me

I share my inner rooms
With you
Not fearing that you tell
My secrets or hate my life.
I open ¾ of rooms completely
Sharing my words with you.
I like talking with you
We stay a few hours on the phone
Then I leave to sleep to wake up to you.

You lie to me…lie to me.
I squeeze the phone in my hand
Asking you why,
And you say "no reason."
I ask you why again
And you say
"You didn't believe me,
I said what you wanted to hear."

## Strongest Female

*I get on that bus:*

*She listens, she's patient*
*She demands my best.*
*She gives without wanting,*
*Asking, anything in return.*
*She's taking a few courses,*
*Pursues, what might be her career*
*And uses her free time to meet me.*

*She's raw with words,*
*We joke a lot.*
*We analyze each other.*
*We don't know when to stop.*
*We always say, "I'm sorry"*
*When the joke hits deeply.*

*She shares her passions*
*But loves to listen to mine.*
*She listens to my day at work,*
*Listens when I'm mad at the world.*
*She worries when I'm hurting,*
*Tries to help by offering advice.*

*I'm leaving this bus, one last time,*
*She's 'the one' I said a few times.*
*Understanding her makes me happy*
*Accepting her strengths inspires me.*
*The bus passes more stops.*
*It arrives at the second last stop.*
*I'm sitting comfy.*
*Before the last stop, I ring the bell,*
*I stand then walk through a crowd,*
*Past females, I relive our relationships.*
*I step down. The bus slows down.*
*I'm ready to get off*

# Mis-Justice

## Bruised Hearts

The sunlight shines on my right
It heats the right leg of my jeans.
In the air, I see no birds flying
In the air, I hear no birds chirping.
On the street, I watch cars passing.
On the sidewalk, I see people walking
On the bridge, I peek over a wooden railing
Knowing that if I went over, I'm dead,
I think about a female, I know.

She's home alone,
She invites her boyfriend over.
They sit on the basement couch
They hit each other, smile,
Then he kisses her.
"You're moving too fast." She says.

He's silent.
He pins her down
Onto the couch.
He drags down her clothes
Then lowers his jeans
And boxers.
He repeatedly pierces her.

I stand. Looking over the railing,
To climb over and fall means death.
I remember listening to her words.
"My mother screams." She says.
She saw 'what he left' in the trash.
"She blames me for inviting him over.
She doesn't want to see my face."
"No one believes me." She says.
"I hate myself!" She yells,
"I want to kill myself!" She ends.

## Can't Find Love In Arguing

He yells, she yells
He yells more.
He pulls his hands back
Extends them forward,
Open palms strike on contact
She falls backwards.
He says, "I'm sorry."

She calls on the phone
He asks, "where were you?"
She doesn't answer, they argue.
He hangs up, doesn't call back.

She eats a box of ice cream
With her best friend
Cause he's mad at her.
They eat the ice cream
Every time he is mad at her.

They discuss how he
Doesn't want, any guy
At school, to talk to her.
How he becomes mad
When he hears
Of any guy talking to her.

*They argue.*
*He pushes her.*
*She falls downstairs*
*About five or six steps.*
*He chases her*
*And says, "I'm sorry."*

# Escape

I did listen to everyone
And did what they said.
Many of them
Formed stories that confuse
Blind and derail my motion.
Many, without useful help
Spoke impatiently as if
They could heal my sight.

I did listen to him
But ½ of what he spoke
Produced and controlled,
How I suffered, what I lost
And added more questions.
I did listen to him
Wanting his words to be true
And what is true will heal him.
There's pressure in guarding the truth
And this can make a powerful man
Act stubborn and motionless.

## Who I Am

*I don't avoid her tears*
*I listen and expand how she feels*

*I don't bury her pain*
*I write the language of a crying heart*

*I don't wrestle with flesh or blood*
*I speak spirit to spirit.*

# Unloving

A man changes who he is,
Not by improving himself
But by lying to the world,
He retains his new image
And what he does.
He meets a female, likes her
Gives this world to her,
His job, his achievements
And his struggles.
They marry.

After years of watching,
She decodes his job
His achievements
His struggles
And nothing is real.
She finds the real him
And confronts him
He denies it
She files for a divorce.

She's afraid unloved.

*Heavier and heavier*
*She smashes her figure,*
*Decides no man will deceive her.*
*Decides to take pleasure from strangers*
*She wants rough hot affection*
*From faceless no ones.*

*'They' amuse her with chatter*
*Never want to listen to her*
*Or want to hold her,*
*'They' excite themselves*

## Unloved Cargo

He comes offering a world
And wants to give it to her.
He offers love and family
Rough pleasure and income security.

She accepts his words,
Overwhelmed by his world
Fantasizes about his promises.
Changes her world
To absorb his thoughts,
She accepts his proposal
They marry.

They can't have children
Years of trying.
She didn't see his temper
Every time he's upset he yells
"No one will love you but me."
She finds his secret, a hidden life.
He didn't work where he said,
Wasn't doing what he claimed.
She left and divorced him.

He comes offering a world.
He mastered its appearance
And doesn't give it to her.
He gives pain and separation
Rough pleasure and cash insecurity.

# Obesity

Chest, heart beat pummmmmping
Flesh covers mattress that lies on the floor.
Physical pain in moving, unable to stand, job lost,
Isolated in a room, can't see the world outside.
A nurse feeds and maintains her flesh.
Her flesh talks faintly,
"I need help...to lose weight."

# BETRAYAL

*His wife gossips,*
*Criticizes his lack of money*
*Complains against his ideas*
*And asks to borrow money*
*From her family,*
*After the bills are unpaid.*
*She opposes his job's worth.*
*Listening ladies condemn him*
*And reject his livelihood.*

*Financially,*
*He gives his wife very little.*
*He craves to carve his purpose*
*By pushing the plans he decides.*
*He tries to get more clients*
*Tries to go to the United States*
*To acquire contracts to work,*
*He arranges payment plans*
*For existing not paying clients.*
*But the tension tightly tightens*
*Cause ladies condemn his efforts.*

He verbally lashes his wife,
Divides their shelter into two parts.
His section is unavailable by a locked door
His interaction with his wife is small.
He sees her before he goes out for work.
He discontinues giving any money
Freezes his will to help his family,
He doesn't speak to his two children.

## Curse and be Cursed

Perry is fired today.
He watches the time
To see if I will be
Fired too.

A week later
Perry calls me and asks
About my job and the others,
Only he is jobless.

Perry wants my job stolen.
Thinks he is a better worker.

Perry, I hold no flame
Under your name,
Find a new job.

Perry we all lose
But you
Should stop here.
Don't call your friend asking,
"Are you still working?"

Think of your wife your son,
A new way to support them.
Think of the travelling distance
It's far. You can work closer.

*Perry I hear you again*
*You say, "Give me a call*
*When you get this."*
*Perry, get a job.*
*Leave my number alone.*

# An Employee's Struggle

Bedtime passing, I won't stop
Wake up early, I won't drop.
Writing working building, job lost
I won't work nights, for any cost.
Didn't like the last job but need a lot
Employee angry now he's stuck.

# Never

Even when rumours start,
The lies blend with the truth
By those who can't stand me
To those who know me.
I'll never accept suicide.

Even when bills smother
A stack of past due notices.
I'm sending resumes out
My wallet is empty.
I'll never accept suicide.

Even when publishers reject me,
Take no risk to lift the industry.
Spend no time to grow with me.
I'll never accept suicide,
I'll fight and continue living.

# IF I MUST PT2

*If I must die*
*Let it not be in darkness*
*Let the light shine*
*And whoever takes my life*
*Let their child forever*
*Be blind by darkness.*

*If I must die*
*Let me see first,*
*Strong dreamers freed*
*From their harness*
*Able to produce*
*And travel to any province,*
*Please, let the educated be free.*

*If I must die*
*Let it be known*
*I wait to go home,*
*Earn what you want*
*Don't crush what another has,*
*Education does begin with parents*
*And then society steals it from us.*
*So if I must die,*
*In protecting what I have*
*Please, let me always have this dream.*

# Emergency Alert

Canada and America
Listen:

Single females raising children
Isn't working,
She's at school studying
After school she's working,
At home she's reviewing,
Her mom is babysitting.

As her son grows older
She tries to ground him.
I mean give him the balance
He needs to face against the world.
So instead of falling, he'll adjust to struggles,
Instead of being lost, he'll protect what he is,
Instead of accepting all, he'll oppose ideas.

# Lost

On her walk to school, thinking
Motherhood arrives, thinking
Stop working to raise my daughter, thinking
If he leaves me, it's hard to support her alone.
Will he stay beside me?
Will he forget his personal dreams?
Will he be a man and provide us with
Money to pay for shelter and security?

On his walk to work, thinking
I'm a father. Things must change! Thinking
Won't go to college, spend time with her. Thinking
First and last month's rent is hard to earn alone.
Will she love someone else during the day?
Will she keep her job and nourish my daughter?
Will she live with us for a year
And not give any checks to help with rent?

## Enough Space

We are helpful, selfish, and proud
We are willing, weak, and brave
We can have any occupation
But only after we are able to see
There is enough space for you and me.

We are diverse, young and strong
Thought sharing, trustworthy
Belief holding, book reading
Hard working workers.
We will be wise workers
After we unite 'educated' ones,
These ones will create a way out.

# Maturity

Saved money
But wallet empty,
For three weeks
Not working.

Email resumes
In bunches
And no return emails
Or calls, no interviews.
I always avoid
Working nights.

On my mind
A short term relief,
Take whatever to fund
The operations,
Further my goals.

The phone rings!
An employer offers
A midnight position,
"No thanks. Bye."

I call her back
Accept the position.
I start tomorrow.

## Fear Exposed

Midnight, moonlight, ambition shines bright
Not working, this way, rest of my life.

Supervisor forces the workers
To bend, kneel, and crawl by a stick
It's sick, how thick the fear of losing a job is.
How these workers so nervous make mistakes
When he is near, and stop talking before he passes.

He tags, knows their name, those who fear him
And uses the fear of termination to intimidate others.

Decent-family supporting-breathers
Bend to his kingdom, kneel for income
Crawl by command, stare at his hand.

They moan, "no talking,
No washroom breaks before lunch."
I ask. "When is lunch?"
They moan. "Three hours away."

I don't ask the supervisor,
I go to the washroom.
I return and see him there.
I approach him. I stand.
Silence.
He's working on my duties.
I say "thanks" and he leaves.

# Survivor

Instead of a windless forest
With direct sunlight
And creeping creatures
Underneath a wet fallen leaf.

Focus on people
The villains the victims,
The mistakes lovers make.
But a few magazines
Reject, won't publish me.
What is it, "I'm outspoken,
Not accepting landscape poetry."
It's difficult to be kind to all
So I won't, but I try and I survive.
And to him who is quietly against me
When the time is set,
"Forget you."

## An Ear for Writing

Conscience hugs the purpose of writing
A rescue, a ringing phone, a loud tone,
Nonsense to the heart without a heart beat
Writing, like breathing, is pure as whole wheat.

Eliminate agencies that move people like cargo.
Adult females won't use the washroom,
Hate their boss he supervises with fear.
This writing rescues. I'm a sensitive ear.

# Cruelty

*Employer thinks:*

Employees beg for their jobs.
Their pleas are nothing
I replace them easily.
I am production, operation.

I sustain law through fear, through cursing.
My tongue convicts anyone outside my order.
I sentence families to weeks of starvation,
I ruin lives through one phrase,
"Don't come back tomorrow."

I don't dress differently. I blend in.
They look for me, pretending to be active
But when I am near, they flee my presence.
I remove all smiles. All talking ceases.

This one, I hate his face
He smiles under my protection.
I hear that he refuses to fear me.
He chats to other employees
And when I arrive. He continues.
This one does not turn and flee
He inspires and creates smiles.
I look directly at him
To deflate his strength.
He stares with greater determination.

I must take his spirit
I'll crush it in my hand.

I speak to him, face to face
My harshest words I say to him.
He talks back! He demands respect.
Other employees arrive like insects,
So I dismiss him. I abolish all inspiration.
He answers again! He demands fairness.
His spirit shines in my presence.
He leaves. A hero to them!
So I follow and rehire him.

I order an employee to watch him,
Study his words and report them.
I'll trap him and fire him.

# Footprints

Prefer to write instead of lifting,
To show a world in each poem.

  Arriving at physical work.

I lift boxes up to my chest
Toss them onto a moving belt,
Wipe the sweat from my forehead
Look at the other males, sweatless.
Take a box cutter and open plastics,
Drop the plastics into another bag.
Unload a second skid,
Thinking about going home,
Will stay until home time.

  Leaving physical work.

Prefer to write instead of lifting,
These poems make footprints in the sand.
My desire is to be far from tossing boxes,
I try to resolve this ongoing debate.
I'll fight through this war
To go where I am to be.

## Inside the World

A young man consumes books,
He travels to different libraries
Enlarges his circumference.
He swallows all-man's prophecy
And rests inside the world.
He attempts to leave the world,
His ears hear the warnings
His eyes see the massive deaths.

A young man digests the internet
And the world fastens assurances
Onto the surface of his mind.
He thinks, 'in knowing I'm free.'
He discredits all things
Until one of his books proves it.
He accepts all-man's stories,
He lives to memorize facts.
He sleeps inside the world.

# Is This Wrong?

*Educated in his country,*
*He comes to Canada.*

*He works $17 an hour*
*Dealing with electronics*
*At the CN Tower.*
*He loses his job*
*After he refuses several times*
*To train his boss's friend,*
*Who will replace him*
*After completing the training.*

*He applies to several jobs*
*No responses,*
*He uses his savings*
*And opens a computer business.*

*Seven years of failure*
*Little local response,*
*He says,*
*"People don't trust me*
*To fix their computers."*

*He closes his business,*
*Goes to an agency.*
*He earns $8.50 an hour*
*Lifting wired trays 8 hours a day.*

**68**

# Sabotage

*Father thinks:*

My ex wife drains my son.
She calls him on his cell
Demands him to skip classes,
Orders him to pay late bills.
He leaves classes
Goes to the bank.
On his drive back,
She calls with a new order.
He doesn't return to his classes.

Nightly, when he's doing homework
She comes to him, demands food.
He leaves his homework
And goes to the 24-hour store.

My son drops out.

My son returns a year later,
He completes his assignments
Passes all his classes.
Teachers encourage him to apply.
He asks me for money for college
I reply. "Tell me when."
Just before the deadline comes
I spend the money on furniture.
He misses his entire first year.

# The Second Ride

## Peaceful Times

Camels drinking before their journey
Their mouths descend inside fresh water
There is no authority around them,
Their riders stumble into the shop
They're laughing, talking and early.
They leave the two camels to drink.

Quickly transporting their riders,
The camels will travel city to city
Drinking fresh water once there,
Never tied, able to rub each other
And find shade when it's hot.

After drinking they raise their heads,
They see different camels, some drinking,
Others wait while tied to wooden poles.

They move to the tied camels.
They rub each one,
They rub their opposite,
Then they go to find shade.

*True Times*

*Their riders stumble outside*
*Moving towards the shade,*
*They mount their camels*
*And lead them out the city.*

*The camels move slowly.*
*The riders want quickness.*

*The camels enter a new city late.*
*Their riders dismount and*
*Unsaddle them.*
*Drags one camel into a dark barn*
*And ties him there.*
*The other rider drags the second camel*
*To a wooden pole and ties her there.*
*Their riders yell and curse*
*While holding money in their hands,*
*They walk into the shop.*